BEST OF
Berlin

★ ★ ★ ★ ★

INHALT
CONTENTS

Die historische Mitte
The Historic Centre
Mitte

4|5

Die neue Mitte
The New Centre
Tiergarten, Moabit

34|35

Rund um die Mitte
Around the Centre
Gesundbrunnen, Prenzlauer Berg, Friedrichshain, Kreuzberg, Tempelhof

60|61

Der Westen
The West
Charlottenburg, Wilmersdorf, Westend, Schöneberg, Dahlem

76|77

Außenbezirke und Potsdam
Suburbs and Potsdam
Köpenick, Treptow, Weißensee, Wannsee, Potsdam

90|91

REGISTER | INDEX   102
BILDNACHWEIS | PHOTO CREDITS   103
IMPRESSUM | IMPRINT   104

Die historische Mitte
The Historic Centre

Der Stadtteil Mitte war immer und ist heute wieder das Zentrum Berlins. Hier stand über Jahrhunderte hinweg das Stadtschloss der Hohenzollern, der preußischen Herrscher. Der Prachtboulevard Unter den Linden verband es mit dem Brandenburger Tor, das den westlichen Abschluss des historischen Stadtkerns bildet. Nach dem Zweiten Weltkrieg lag Berlin in Schutt und Asche und wurde in vier Sektoren aufgeteilt. Der Stadtteil Mitte mit den östlich angrenzenden Bezirken wurde ab 1949 zu »Berlin, Hauptstadt der DDR«. Die Errichtung der Mauer 1961 zementierte die Teilung der Stadt. Rund um den Alexanderplatz entstand von 1964 bis 1971 ein neues Zentrum, West-Berlin hingegen fand jenseits des Tiergartens statt. Nach der Wiedervereinigung wurde in der historischen Mitte über zwei Jahrzehnte hinweg vieles saniert oder wiederaufgebaut, ein Prozess, der immer noch nicht abgeschlossen ist.

The Mitte district was always and today is once again the centre of Berlin. For centuries the Stadtschloss, the city palace of the Hohenzollern dynasty, the rulers of Prussia, stood here. The magnificent boulevard Unter den Linden connected it to the Brandenburg Gate, at the western end of the historic city centre. After the Second World War, Berlin lay in ruins and was divided into four sectors. Mitte and the districts bordering it to the east became »Berlin, capital of the GDR« in 1949. The construction of the Berlin Wall in 1961 sealed the partition of the city. A new centre grew up around Alexanderplatz between 1964 and 1971, while the life of West Berlin took place on the other side of the Tiergarten park. After reunification much of the historic Mitte district was restored or rebuilt over a period of two decades, a process that has still not been completed.

Das Brandenburger Tor ist das weltberühmte Wahrzeichen Berlins. Seit 1793 hat die Quadriga die Geschichte der Stadt miterlebt.

The Brandenburg Gate is the world-famous emblem of Berlin. Since 1793 the Quadriga has witnessed the history of the city.

Der Pariser Platz vor dem Brandenburger » Tor: Seine Neubebauung nach dem Mauerfall basierte auf den Besitzverhältnissen vor dem Ersten Weltkrieg – mit britischer, französischer und amerikanischer Botschaft, dem Hotel Adlon und der Akademie der Künste.

Pariser Platz in front of the Brandenburg Gate: its reconstruction after the fall of the Wall was based on ownership before the First World War – with the British, French and American embassies, the Hotel Adlon and the Academy of Arts.

Das Adlon, als kaiserliches Prunkhotel 1907 » eröffnet, brannte im Zweiten Weltkrieg aus. Der Fünf-Sterne-Plus-Palast ist auch heute wieder erste Adresse für gekrönte und ungekrönte Häupter dieser Welt.

The Adlon, an imperial grand hotel that opened in 1907, burnt down in the Second World War. Today this five-star-plus palace is once again the top address for royalty and other celebrated persons.

Von außen unauffällig, im Inneren atembe- › raubend: Die DZ Bank auf der Südseite des Pariser Platzes stammt vom weltbekannten Stararchitekten Frank O. Gehry.

Inconspicuous from outside, breathtaking within: the DZ Bank on the south side of Pariser Platz was designed by the world-famous architect Frank O. Gehry.

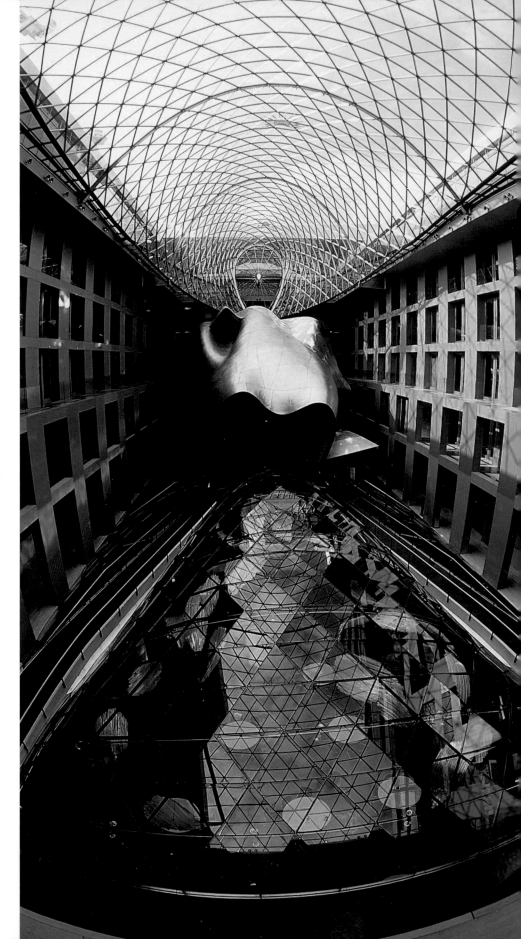

Das im Jahr 2005 eingeweihte Denkmal für ›
die ermordeten Juden Europas, oft kurz
Holocaust-Mahnmal genannt, ist eine ge-
wellte Landschaft aus 2700 unterschiedlich
hohen Betonstelen, zwischen denen man
sich verlieren kann: »Ohne Anfang und
ohne Ende, ohne Eingang und ohne Aus-
gang«, so der amerikanische Architekt Peter Eisenman.

The Memorial to the Murdered Jews of Europe, often known for short as the Holo-
caust Memorial, was unveiled in 2005. It is
an undulating landscape of 2,700 concrete
slabs of varying height, among which visitors can get lost: »Without beginning and
end, without entrance and exit«, according
to its American architect Peter Eisenman.

‹ Auf Initiative von Wilhelm von Humboldt wurde mit der heutigen Humboldt-Universität 1809 die erste Universität Berlins gegründet. Sein Bruder Alexander, hier dessen Standbild von Reinhold Begas, war ein bedeutender Weltreisender und Naturforscher.

Berlin's first university, today called the Humboldt-Universität, was founded in 1809 on the initiative of Wilhelm von Humboldt. His brother (Alexander), whose statue by Reinhold Begas is shown here, was a prominent explorer and researcher of nature.

‹ Das barocke, im frühen 18. Jahrhundert vollendete Zeughaus ist das älteste Gebäude am Prachtboulevard Unter den Linden. Heute befindet sich in dem als Waffenarsenal errichteten Gebäude das Deutsche Historische Museum.

The Baroque Zeughaus, completed in the early 18th century, is the oldest building on the boulevard Unter den Linden. Built as an arsenal, the building is now the home of the Deutsches Historisches Museum.

‹ Die Schlossbrückenskulpturen bilden einen starken Kontrast zur Friedrichswerderschen Kirche von Karl Friedrich Schinkel (vollendet 1830), die heute als Museum dient.

The sculptures on the Schlossbrücke contrast strongly with the Friedrichswerdersche Kirche, a church completed by Karl Friedrich Schinkel in 1830, which is now a museum.

« Alt und neu in aufregendem Mix: Im Rücken des barocken Zeughauses liegt der gläserne Erweiterungsbau von I. M. Pei.

An exciting blend of old and new: at the rear of the Baroque-style Zeughaus lies the glass extension designed by I. M. Pei.

‹ Die katholische St.-Hedwigs-Kathedrale, erbaut um 1750, ist Teil des Forum Fridericianum rund um den heutigen Bebelplatz.

The Catholic Cathedral of St Hedwig, built in about 1750, is part of the Forum Fridericianum around the square now called Bebelplatz.

⌐ Die Neue Wache (1818) stammt von Karl Friedrich Schinkel. Das Wachhäuschen wurde nach dem Mauerfall zur Gedenkstätte für die Opfer von Krieg und Gewaltherrschaft.

The Neue Wache (1818) is the work of Karl Friedrich Schinkel. After the fall of the Berlin Wall, this guardhouse became a place of memorial for the victims of war and tyranny.

⌐ Unter der Deckenöffnung der Neuen Wache sitzt die vergrößerte »Pietà« der Bildhauerin und Malerin Käthe Kollwitz.

Below the opening in the roof of the Neue Wache stands the »Pietà« by the sculptor and painter Käthe Kollwitz.

⌃ Der Bebelplatz mit der Alten Bibliothek am Prachtboulevard Unter den Linden gehört zu den schönsten Plätzen der Hauptstadt.

Bebelplatz, the site of the Alte Bibliothek on the grand boulevard Unter den Linden, is one of the most attractive squares in the city.

‹ Die Humboldt-Box ist Berlins neuestes temporäres Wahrzeichen. Sie zeigt Pläne und Vorhaben rund um den Wiederaufbau des Stadtschlosses als Humboldt-Forum.

The Humboldt-Box is Berlin's latest temporary landmark. It holds an exhibition of plans and projects associated with the reconstruction of the Stadtschloss, which will be called Humboldt-Forum.

‹ Vom Berliner Dom aus bietet sich ein weiter Blick auf das Grün des Lustgartens.

From the Protestant cathedral, Berliner Dom, there is a broad view of the greenery in the Lustgarten.

‹ Der bronzene »Löwenkämpfer« (1861) im Lustgarten wurde nach einem Entwurf von Christian Daniel Rauch gefertigt.

The bronze »Lion Tamer« (1861) in the Lustgarten was cast to a design by Christian Daniel Rauch.

« Den Berliner Dom gab Kaiser Wilhelm II. als Hof- und Denkmalskirche der Hohenzollern sowie als Hauptsitz des preußischen Protestantismus in Auftrag. Er wurde 1905 geweiht.

Emperor Wilhelm II commissioned the Berliner Dom to be the court and memorial church of the Hohenzollern dynasty and the principal seat of Prussian Protestantism. It was inaugurated in 1905.

Das Alte Museum von Karl Friedrich Schin- ≈
kel (1830) war eines der ersten öffentlichen
Museen Deutschlands. Als Teil der Museumsinsel gehört es zum Unesco-Welterbe.

The Altes Museum, designed by Karl Friedrich Schinkel (1830), was one of Germany's
first public museums. It is part of the Museum Island, a Unesco World Heritage site.

Das 1904 eröffnete Bode-Museum bildet ⌃
mit seiner weithin sichtbaren Kuppel den
nördlichen Abschluss der Museumsinsel.

The Bode-Museum, which opened in 1904,
marks the north end of the Museum Island
with its eye-catching dome.

Die 1876 fertiggestellte Alte Nationalgalerie ⟩
beherbergt heute die Kunstsammlungen
des 19. Jahrhunderts auf der Museumsinsel.

The Alte Nationalgalerie was completed in
1876. It is now home to collections of 19th-
century art on the Museum Island.

‹ Der Pergamonaltar im gleichnamigen Museum: Für ihn und andere weltweit bedeutende historische Architekturen wurde der 1909 bis 1930 errichtete Museumsbau maßgeschneidert – einmalig in Europa.

The Pergamon Altar in the museum of the same name: it was purpose-built between 1909 and 1930 to house the altar and other historic architecture of global significance – something unique in Europe.

Die im Neuen Museum auf der Museums- ›
insel aufbewahrte Büste der Nofretete zählt
zu den bekanntesten Kunstschätzen des
Alten Ägypten und gilt als Meisterwerk der
Bildhauerkunst aus der Amarna-Zeit.

The bust of Nofretete displayed in the Neues Museum on the Museum Island, a masterpiece of sculpture from the Amarna period, is one of the most famous treasures of
ancient Egypt.

Das um 1850 entstandene Neue Museum »
war seit dem Zweiten Weltkrieg eine Ruine.
Von dem britischen Stararchitekten David
Chipperfield aufwendig restauriert und
wiederhergestellt, wurde es 2009 wiedereröffnet.

After the Second World War the Neues Museum, dating from about 1850, was a ruin.
Restored and reconstructed at great expense by the British star architect David
Chipperfield, it reopened in 2009.

‹ Die Weltzeituhr auf dem Alexanderplatz galt den Ost-Berlinern als beliebter Treffpunkt. Der dahinter aufragende Fernsehturm aus den 1960er-Jahren ist mit 368 Metern das höchste Bauwerk Deutschlands.

The World Clock on Alexanderplatz was a popular rendezvous for East Berliners. At 368 metres, the 1960s television tower that rises behind it is the tallest building in Germany.

« Das Rote Rathaus ist Sitz des Regierenden Bürgermeisters von Berlin. Der Name bezieht sich auf die Ziegelsteinfassade des Gebäudes. Reinhold Begas' Neptunbrunnen stand ursprünglich vor dem Stadtschloss.

The Rotes Rathaus is the seat of the Governing Mayor of Berlin. The name, meaning red town hall, derives from the brick façade of the building. The Neptune Fountain by Reinhold Begas originally stood in front of the Stadtschloss.

❮ Das Nikolaiviertel, Berlins ältestes Wohnge-
biet, wurde zur 750-Jahr-Feier der Stadt im
Jahr 1987 historisierend rekonstruiert.

The Nikolaiviertel, Berlin's oldest residential
quarter, was rebuilt in historic style for the
750th anniversary of the city in 1987.

❮ Das 1765 erbaute Ephraim-Palais mit seinen
zarten Rokoko-Details galt immer schon als
die »schönste Ecke Berlins«. In den 1930er-
Jahren wegen Bauarbeiten komplett abge-
tragen, lagerten die durchnummerierten
Fassadenteile bis 1983 im Westteil der Stadt.

The Ephraim-Palais of 1765 with its delicate
Rococo details has always been regarded as
»the prettiest corner of Berlin«. In the 1930s
it was completely removed for building
work, and the numbered parts of its façade
remained in West Berlin until 1983.

❮ Bummeln im Nikolaiviertel: Die Skulptur des
Hl. Georg (1853) von August Kiss stand ursprünglich im Hof des Stadtschlosses.

A stroll through the Nikolaiviertel: the sculpture of St George (1853) by August Kiss originally stood in the courtyard of the Stadtschloss.

❮❮ Die Nikolaikirche ist heute Museum für Berliner Geschichte bis zum Dreißigjährigen
Krieg. 1539 wurde hier die Reformation ein-
geführt.

The Nikolaikirche is now a museum of the
history of Berlin up to the Thirty Years' War.
In 1539 the Reformation was introduced to
this church.

Weithin sichtbar sind die goldenen Kup- ›
peln der Neuen Synagoge in der Oranienburger Straße, des ehemals größten jüdischen Gotteshauses in Berlin.

The golden domes of the Neue Synagoge
in Oranienburger Strasse, once the largest
Jewish place of worship in Berlin, are visible
from afar.

Die Hackeschen Höfe in bühnenreifer Art- »
déco-Pracht: Das Areal mit seinen acht Innenhöfen ist ein touristischer Magnet in der
Hauptstadt.

The Hackesche Höfe are a magnificent Art
Deco stage set and, with their eight courtyards, a magnet for tourists in the German
capital.

Der Friedrichstadt-Palast aus den frühen ≫
1980er-Jahren bot schon zu DDR-Zeiten
opulente Ausstattungsrevuen.

The Friedrichstadt-Palast, built in the early
1980s, put on splendid variety shows even
in the GDR years.

Das Quartier 206 bietet cooles Nobelshop- ∧
ping über mehrere Etagen.

Quartier 206 is a place for cool, exclusive
shopping over several storeys.

Galt die Friedrichstraße den Berlinern bis ›
zum Zweiten Weltkrieg als Ausgehmeile, ist
sie heute Einkaufsstraße – dicht bepackt
mit trendigen Shops und Kaufhäusern.

An entertainment district for the people of
Berlin before the Second World War, Fried-
richstrasse is a shopping street today – one
trendy outlet and department store next to
another.

‹ Die Kuppeltürme der beiden Dome auf dem Gendarmenmarkt wurden unter Friedrich II. nach Plänen von Carl von Gontard errichtet. Im Vordergrund das Schillerdenkmal von Reinhold Begas (Einweihung 1871).

The domed towers of the two churches on Gendarmenmarkt were built to plans by Carl von Gontard during the reign of Friedrich II. In the foreground is the monument to Schiller by Reinhold Begas, inaugurated in 1871.

⌃ Der Gendarmenmarkt mit dem Schauspielhaus von Karl Friedrich Schinkel (1820; jetzt Konzerthaus Berlin) ist die wohl schönste Platzanlage der Hauptstadt. Links steht der Deutsche, rechts der Französische Dom.

Gendarmenmarkt with the theatre designed by Karl Friedrich Schinkel (1820; now the Konzerthaus Berlin) is probably the most beautiful square in the city. The churches are the Deutscher Dom on the left and the Französischer Dom on the right.

⌃ Das Innere des Deutschen Doms wurde bis in die Krone hinein entkernt. Hier ist seit 2002 die Dauerausstellung des Deutschen Bundestages »Wege – Irrwege – Umwege« zu sehen.

The interior of the Deutscher Dom was stripped bare up to the ceiling of the cupola. Since 2002 it has been home to a permanent exhibition on parliamentarianism in Germany, initiated by the Bundestag, the German parliament.

Die kleinteilige, bunte Rekonstruktion einer ˄ alten Berliner Mietshaus-Reihung stammt von dem italienischen Stararchitekten Aldo Rossi. Das Ensemble hat die Zimmerstraße im alten Zeitungsviertel ordentlich aufgewertet.

This small-scale, colourful reconstruction of a row of old Berlin tenements is the work of the eminent Italian architect Aldo Rossi. The ensemble represents a considerable upgrade for Zimmerstrasse in the old newspaper quarter.

Der Checkpoint Charlie war nach dem Mau- › erbau 1961 die einzige Übergangsstelle nach Ost-Berlin für Alliierte Streitkräfte, Ausländer und Diplomaten. Auf dem Höhepunkt des Kalten Krieges standen sich hier amerikanische und russische Panzer gegenüber. Auch der eine oder andere Spion hat hier die Seiten gewechselt.

After construction of the Berlin Wall in 1961, Checkpoint Charlie was the only crossing point to East Berlin for Allied soldiers, foreigners and diplomats. At the height of the Cold War, American and Russian tanks confronted each other, and more than one spy changed sides here.

Die neue Mitte
The New Centre

Nördlich und südlich des Brandenburger Tors, am Rande des Tiergartens, sind die Trümmerlandschaften des Zweiten Weltkriegs über Jahrzehnte hinweg liegen geblieben, immer hart entlang des Mauerverlaufs, mäandernd zwischen Ost und West. Nach der Wende entstand rund um das alte neue Reichstagsgebäude, seit 1999 Sitz des gesamtdeutschen Parlaments, das »Band des Bundes« mit den Regierungsbauten und dem gigantischen Kanzleramt. Am Tiergartenrand erwachte das alte Diplomatenviertel mit zahlreichen Botschaftsbauten zu neuem Leben, am Potsdamer Platz entstand ein völlig neues Hochhaus-, Wohn- und Vergnügungsviertel und nördlich der Spree ragt der riesige gläserne Hauptbahnhof in den Himmel: Willkommen im neuen Herz Berlins.

North and south of the Brandenburg Gate, at the edge of the Tiergarten, landscapes of rubble from the Second World War remained for decades – close by the course of the Wall meandering between East and West. After German reunification the »Band des Bundes«, a band of federal government buildings, was constructed around the old, renovated Reichstag building, since 1999 the seat of the German parliament. One of them is the huge Chancellery. At the borders of the Tiergarten, new life was breathed into the old diplomatic quarter with its many embassies. Potsdamer Platz is an entirely new district of skyscrapers, housing and places of entertainment, and north of the river Spree rises the enormous glass structure of the new Hauptbahnhof, the main station. Welcome to the new heart of Berlin.

Touristenmagnet: Blick in die gläserne Kuppel des Reichstagsgebäudes, dem Sitz des Deutschen Bundestages. ›

A magnet for tourists: a glimpse inside the glass dome of the Reichstag, seat of the Deutscher Bundestag.

‹ Transparenz: Die lichtdurchflutete Kuppel von Sir Norman Foster ist über ein Spiralband begehbar und bietet Blicke nach innen wie nach außen.

Transparency: flooded with light, Sir Norman Foster's dome is accessible via a spiral walkway, providing views inside and outside the building.

‹ Im Innern der Reichstagskuppel leiten 360 trichterförmig angeordnete Spiegel Tageslicht in den darunterliegenden Plenarsaal.

Within the dome of the Reichstag, 360 mirrors arranged in the shape of a funnel transmit daylight into the parliament chamber below.

‹ Durch ein Glasdach können die Besucher der Kuppel in den Plenarsaal schauen.

Through a glass ceiling, visitors can look down from the dome into the parliament chamber.

« Jeder Besucher Berlins möchte das von Sir Norman Foster sanierte alte Reichstagsgebäude erleben. Von einem der Fenster am Hauptportal wurde am 9. November 1918 die Republik ausgerufen.

Every visitor to Berlin wants to see the old Reichstag building that was renovated by Sir Norman Foster. On 9 November 1918 the foundation of a republic was proclaimed from one of the windows at the main entrance.

Das »Band des Bundes«: Die Regierungs- ≋
bauten verbinden als architektonisches
Band die Ufer des Spreebogens – und so
symbolisch Ost- mit West-Berlin, die einstige DDR mit der BRD.

The buildings of the federal government
are like an architectural ribbon linking the
two banks of the bend in the Spree – and
thus symbolically connecting East and
West Berlin, the GDR of the past with the
Federal Republic.

Bei schönem Wetter tummeln sich Genie- ⌃
ßer auf den Liegewiesen, an den Stränden
und in den Cafés entlang der Spree.

In sunny weather, leisure-seekers flock to
the lawns, beaches and cafés along the
Spree.

Vor der Repräsentationsarchitektur des ⟩
Bundeskanzleramtes wirkt sogar die Skulptur »Berlin« von Eduardo Chillada zierlich.

Against the backdrop of the imposing architecture of the Federal Chancellery, even
Eduardo Chillada's sculpture »Berlin« looks
dainty.

DIE NEUE MITTE | THE NEW CENTRE

» Der einstige Hamburger Bahnhof, entkernt, saniert und erweitert, ist heute das Museum für Gegenwartskunst der Staatlichen Museen zu Berlin.

A disused rail station, the Hamburger Bahnhof, now renovated from top to bottom and extended, is dedicated to contemporary art and is one of the Staatliche Museen zu Berlin.

» In der Nähe des Regierungsviertels steht der 2006 eröffnete gläserne Superbau des neuen Hauptbahnhofs der Architekten Gerkan, Marg & Partner.

The spectacular glass structure of the Hauptbahnhof by the architects Gerkan, Marg & Partner, opened in 2006, lies close to the government district.

‹ Weithin sichtbar ist das Spreebogencenter in Moabit: Eyecatcher der Bebauung ist das Bundesinnenministerium mit seinen zwei abgerundeten Turmblöcken.

The Spreebogencenter in Moabit is highly visible: the building's striking feature is the Federal Ministry of the Interior with its two rounded towers.

‹ Die Siegessäule im Zentrum des Großen Sterns erinnert unter anderem an den Sieg über Frankreich im Jahre 1871; die strahlende Siegesgöttin Viktoria haben die Berliner »Goldelse« getauft.

The Siegessäule at the centre of the Grosser Stern commemorates the defeat of France in 1871; the Berliners' name for the shining goddess of victory is »Goldelse«.

⌃ Das Haus der Kulturen der Welt liegt rückseitig romantisch an der Spree. Ursprünglich als Kongresshalle errichtet, war der schwungvolle Bau von 1957 ein Geschenk der Amerikaner an West-Berlin.

The Haus der Kulturen der Welt has a romantic location on the Spree to the rear; this curved structure, originally built as a congress hall, was a donation of the United States of America to West Berlin in 1957.

⌃ Das Sowjetische Ehrenmal war das erste neue Bauwerk nach Kriegsende 1945, errichtet aus Granit und Marmorblöcken der zerstörten Reichskanzlei Adolf Hitlers. Es ehrt die 80 000 Soldaten der Roten Armee, die im Kampf um Berlin gefallen sind.

The Soviet Memorial, the first new structure built after the end of the war in 1945, was made from granite and blocks of marble taken from Adolf Hitler's ruined Reichkanzlei (Chancellery). It honours the 80,000 soldiers of the Red Army who died in the battle for Berlin.

Berlinale: In den Kinos auf dem Areal des ⊗ Potsdamer Platzes trifft sich die internationale Filmwelt.

The Berlinale: for this film festival the world of international cinema meets in cinemas on the area of Potsdamer Platz.

Das Debis Haus, 1997 bezogen, stammt von ⌃ Renzo Piano. Das gigantische Atrium hat die Ausmaße einer Kathedrale.

The Debis Haus, inaugurated in 1997, was designed by Renzo Piano. Its gigantic atrium has cathedral-like dimensions.

Helmut Jahn aus Chicago hat das Sony Center am Potsdamer Platz gebaut – mit dem Forum, einer lichtdurchfluteten offenen Arena mit gefalteter Zeltüberdachung. Hier lustwandelt der Berliner oder nimmt an Großveranstaltungen teil.

Helmut Jahn from Chicago built the Sony Center on Potsdamer Platz – including the Forum, a brightly lit open arena with a folded tent roof. Here the people of Berlin like to stroll or take part in big events.

In den 1920er-Jahren galt der Potsdamer »
Platz als der verkehrsreichste Europas. Der
Uhrenturm mit der Plattform für die Ver-
kehrspolizisten stand inmitten des brau-
senden Gewühls.

In the 1920s Potsdamer Platz was regarded
as the busiest traffic intersection in Europe.
The clock tower with a platform for a traffic
policeman stood in the middle of the roar-
ing melée.

Straßenführung und Platzanlagen – hier »
der Marlene-Dietrich-Platz – entsprechen
in ihrer Dichte und Kompaktheit dem alten
Straßenraster Berlins.

The course of the streets and the siting of
the squares – here Marlene-Dietrich-Platz
– correspond to the old street plan of Berlin
in their density and compactness.

Das Areal des Potsdamer Platzes wurde ›
nach der Wende komplett neu gestaltet.
Die Röhren mit den aufgesetzten Spiegeln
bringen Tageslicht in die unteren Ebenen
des S- und U-Bahnhofes.

The Potsdamer Platz area was completely
remodelled after German reunification. The
pipes clad with mirrors reflect daylight into
the lower levels of the underground and
train station.

^ Blick über den östlichen Tiergarten; im Vordergrund der Potsdamer Platz mit dem Sony-Center.

View across the eastern part of the Tiergarten district, with Potsdamer Platz and Sony Center in the foreground.

Das Kulturforum vereint großartige Einzel- ›
bauten, darunter die Neue Nationalgalerie
von Ludwig Mies van der Rohe (rechts), die
Philharmonie, das Kunstgewerbemuseum
und die Gemäldegalerie.

The Kulturforum combines superb indivi-
dual buildings like the Neue Nationalgalerie by Ludwig Mies van der Rohe, the Philharmonie, the Kunstgewerbemuseum and
the Gemäldegalerie.

Die Philharmonie mit ihren goldschim- ›
mernden Dachspitzen von Hans Scharoun
(1963) ist einer der markantesten Nach-
kriegsbauten in Berlin. Sie ist die Heimat
der Berliner Philharmoniker.

The Philharmonie by Hans Scharoun (1963)
with its pointed roof gleaming golden is
one of Berlin's most striking post-war buildings. It is the home of the Berlin Philhar-
monic Orchestra.

Designklassiker: In den umfangreichen ›
Sammlungen des Kunstgewerbemuseums
findet sich auch modernes Möbeldesign.

Classic design: the extensive applied art
collections of the Kunstgewerbemuseum
include modern furniture.

In der Gemäldegalerie am Kulturforum »
kann man Kunstschätze von Weltruhm be-
wundern.

World-famous paintings can be admired in
the Gemäldegalerie in the Kulturforum.

Weiße, schlank gestaffelte Shedtürme ^
kennzeichnen das Bauhaus-Archiv/Muse-
um für Gestaltung. Walter Gropius, der die
berühmte Ausbildungsstätte 1919 in Weimar gegründet hatte, ist auch der Architekt
dieses Gebäudes aus dem Jahr 1964.

Slender white shed roofs characterise the
Bauhaus-Archiv/Museum für Gestaltung,
an archive and design museum. Walter Gropius, who founded the famous Bauhaus
school in Weimar in 1919, also designed this
building, which dates from 1964.

⌃ Die Gedenkstätte Deutscher Widerstand im Bendlerblock befindet sich auf dem Areal des heutigen Bundesverteidigungsministeriums. Sie ehrt unter anderem die Männer, die nach dem misslungenen Attentat auf Hitler im Juli 1944 hier erschossen wurden.

The German Resistance Memorial Center in the Bendlerblock is situated on what is now the Federal Ministry of Defence. Among the people it commemorates are the men who were shot here after the failed assassination attempt on Hitler in July 1944.

⌃ Im Ehrenhof des Bendlerblocks steht die Statue eines nackten Jünglings mit gebundenen Händen (1953) von Richard Scheibe.

In the courtyard of the Bendlerblock stands a statue of a naked boy with tied hands (1953) by Richard Scheibe.

Im alten Diplomatenviertel sind zahlreiche ⌃ Botschaften beheimatet. Neben sanierten alten Botschaftsbauten stößt man auf viele neue architektonische Highlights wie zum Beispiel die Botschaft Mexikos, die nicht nur bei nächtlicher Beleuchtung beeindruckend ist.

Numerous embassies are located in the old diplomatic quarter. In addition to renovated old embassy buildings, many new architectural highlights can be seen here – for example, the Mexican embassy, which is impressive by day as well as when it is lit up at night.

Die Botschaft des Königreichs der Nieder- ⟩ lande, von den Architekten Rem Koolhaas und Ellen van Loon entworfen, ist international beachtetes und preisgekröntes Gesamtkunstwerk.

The embassy of the Kingdom of the Netherlands, designed by the architects Rem Koolhaas and Ellen van Loon, is an internationally respected and award-winning all-round work of art.

‹ Der Zoologische Garten in Berlin ist einer der größten Europas. Das fernöstlich inspirierte Elefantentor dient als Eingang und liegt an der Grenze des Tiergartens zu Charlottenburg, der City West.

The Zoologischer Garten in Berlin is one of the largest zoos in Europe. The Elephant Gate with its oriental inspiration is the entrance at the border of Tiergarten and Charlottenburg, the western part of the city.

≈ Die Eisbären im Zoologischen Garten zählen zu den Lieblingen der Berliner.

The polar bears are among the Berliners' favourite animals in the Zoologischer Garten.

^ Berlin besitzt auch aufgrund seiner Wasserstraßen viele idyllische Orte, etwa die Hausboote auf dem Flutgraben des Landwehrkanals an der Unterschleuse.

Thanks to its waterways Berlin possesses many idyllic spots, such as the place where houseboats are moored on the flood channel of the Landwehrkanal at the Unterschleuse lock.

‹ Das 1998 vollendete Bundespräsidialamt mit seinem großen, lichtdurchfluteten Atrium bildet einen eleganten Kontrast zum benachbarten Schloss Bellevue.

With its large, well-lit atrium, the Federal President's Office, completed in 1998, makes an elegant contrast to neighbouring Schloss Bellevue.

« Das frühklassizistische Schloss Bellevue aus dem Jahr 1785 in der Nähe des Großen Sterns ist der Amtssitz des Bundespräsidenten.

Schloss Bellevue, built in early Neoclassical style in 1785 near the Grosser Stern, is the official seat of the president of the Federal Republic of Germany.

Rund um die Mitte
Around the Centre

Rund um die historische Mitte liegen die Ortsteile Gesundbrunnen, Prenzlauer Berg, Friedrichshain und Kreuzberg. Hier entstanden nach der Proklamation des Deutschen Kaiserreichs 1871 die Mietskasernenviertel für die rasant wachsende Bevölkerung der Industriemetropole. Nach der Teilung Berlins wurde in den 1950er- und 60er-Jahren in Friedrichshain die Repräsentationsmagistrale der DDR, die Stalinallee, gebaut, die man 1961 in Karl-Marx-Allee umbenannte. Im Westen siedelten sich mit dem Wirtschaftswunder in den 1960er-Jahren besonders in Kreuzberg türkische Gastarbeiter und ihre Familien an und blieben. Seit dem Mauerfall sind auch die östlichen alten Quartiere überaus lebendige und begehrte Wohn- und Geschäftsbezirke.

The districts that surround the historic city centre are Gesundbrunnen, Prenzlauer Berg, Friedrichshain and Kreuzberg. After the foundation of the German Empire in 1871, areas of tenement housing for the rapidly growing population of industrial Berlin sprang up here. In the 1950s and 1960s after the partition of the city, the showcase avenue of the GDR, Stalinallee (renamed Karl-Marx-Allee in 1961) was constructed in Friedrichshain. In West Berlin during the years of the »economic miracle« in the 1960s, Turkish guest workers arrived with their families and stayed, especially in the Kreuzberg district. Since the fall of the Wall the old areas of East Berlin have also become extremely lively and sought-after commercial and residential areas.

Fassaden aus der Zeit um 1900 im Ortsteil › Prenzlauer Berg. Tief gestaffelt mit mehreren Innenhöfen bilden die Mietshäuser der Gründerzeit die Blockstrukturen der alten Wohn- und Gewerbeviertel der Hauptstadt.

Façades from the period around 1900 in the Prenzlauer Berg district. With lines of courtyards, the tenements give a structure to the old residential and industrial quarters of the German capital.

‹ Der Kollwitzplatz in Prenzlauer Berg: Hier treffen sich die Anwohner und Gäste Berlins vom ausgiebigen Frühstück bis zum nächtlichen Absacker.

Kollwitzplatz in Prenzlauer Berg: locals and visitors to Berlin meet here at all times of the day, from a leisurely breakfast to a nightcap.

≫ Während des Mauerbaus 1961 stand die Bernauer Straße – eine Straßenseite West, eine Ost – im Rampenlicht der Weltöffentlichkeit. Im Bereich der heutigen Gedenkstätte Berliner Mauer steht einer ihrer wenigen authentischen, innerstädtischen Reste.

While the Wall was being built in 1961, Bernauer Strasse – one side of it in the West, the other in the East – was exposed to the glare of global publicity. Close to what is now the Berlin Wall Memorial stands one of the few remaining authentic inner-city parts of the Wall.

⌃ Das »Fenster des Gedenkens« der Gedenkstätte Berliner Mauer erinnert mit Porträts an die Menschen, die bei einem Fluchtversuch ums Leben kamen.

The portraits in the »Window of Remembrance« at the Berlin Wall Memorial preserve the memory of people who died while attempting to escape.

» Das Frankfurter Tor ist ein Platz an der Karl-Marx-Allee in Friedrichshain. Der Platzname spiegelt sich in der Architektur der Türme an seiner Westseite wider, die dank ihrer symmetrischen Anordnung wie ein Stadttor wirken.

The Frankfurter Tor is a square on Karl-Marx-Allee in the district of Friedrichshain. The name is reflected in the architecture of the tower blocks on its west side, which look like a gate (Tor) thanks to their symmetrical arrangement.

» Östlich des Alexanderplatzes entstand zwischen 1949 und 1969 der Prachtboulevard, der seit 1961 den Namen Karl-Marx-Allee trägt.

East of Alexanderplatz, between 1949 and 1969, the grand boulevard, which since 1961 has borne the name Karl-Marx-Allee, was built.

‹ Der Baustil der Karl-Marx-Allee ist eine Mischform aus Moskauer Zuckerbäckerstil und preußischem Klassizismus: »Sozialistisch im Inhalt, in der Form national«.

The architecture of Karl-Marx-Allee is a mixture of Moscow »wedding-cake« style and Prussian Neoclassicism: »Socialist in content, national in form«.

Die zahlreichen Flohmärkte Berlins sind ›
Top-Attraktionen; hier das bunte Gewirr auf
dem Boxhagener Platz in Friedrichshain.

Berlin's numerous flea markets are leading
attractions; this is the colourful bustle on
Boxhagener Platz in Friedrichshain.

Die Oberbaumbrücke war seit dem Mauer- ›
bau verbarrikadiert. Heute verbindet sie
wieder die alten, jetzt angesagten Arbeiter-
bezirke Kreuzberg und Friedrichshain.

The Oberbaumbrücke was blocked up after
the building of the Wall. Today this bridge
once again links the old, now fashionable,
working-class districts of Kreuzberg and
Friedrichshain.

East Side Gallery: Das rund ein Kilometer ›
lange, graffitigeschmückte Mauerstück am
Spreeufer steht unter Denkmalschutz.

East Side Gallery: this stretch of the Berlin
Wall on the banks of the Spree, about one
kilometre long and decorated with graffiti,
is a protected monument.

Die 30 Meter hohe Skulptur »Molecule ››
Man« von Jonathan Borowsky steht nahe
der Oberbaumbrücke in der Spree.

Jonathan Borowsky's 30-metre-high sculpture »Molecule Man« stands in the Spree
near the Oberbaumbrücke.

« Die Gedenkstätte Topographie des Terrors – mit großem Ausstellungszentrum – liegt auf dem Gelände der Zentrale des NS-Terrors mit ihren freigelegten Gefängniszellen und Folterkellern.

The memorial Topography of Terror with its large exhibition space is situated in the place where the central organs of Nazi terror had their prison cells and torture chambers, now excavated for public view.

« Einer der größten Fernbahnhöfe Berlins war der Anhalter Bahnhof. Er wurde im Zweiten Weltkrieg stark beschädigt und später abgerissen. Nur noch die Ruine des Portikus erinnert an ihn.

The Anhalter Bahnhof was one of Berlin's main stations for long-distance trains. It was severely damaged in the Second World War and later demolished. Only the ruin of the portico now marks the site.

‹ Der imposante Martin-Gropius-Bau ist heute Veranstaltungsort internationaler Wechselausstellungen. Errichtet wurde er 1881 als Kunstgewerbemuseum.

The imposing Martin-Gropius-Bau is today used for holding international temporary exhibitions. It was built in 1881 as a museum of arts and crafts.

Im anmutigen Barockbau von 1730, dem ⤊ preußischen Kammergericht, saß E. T. A. Hoffmann bei der Arbeit. Seine Romane wurden Höhepunkte der deutschen Romantik. Für die Westhälfte der Stadt wurde das Gebäude dann zum Berlin-Museum.

This graceful Baroque building of 1730, a Prussian court of law, was the place of work of E. T. A. Hoffmann, whose novels were amongst the greatest achievements of German Romanticism. For the western half of the city, this building later became the Berlin-Museum.

Heute ist der Barockbau Teil des von Daniel ⌃ Libeskind entworfenen Jüdischen Museums. Die spröden Umrisse eines zerborstenen Davidsterns bilden ein Zickzackband, das sich symbolisch durch die Berliner Stadtgeschichte zieht.

Today the Baroque structure is part of the Jewish Museum, which was designed by Daniel Libeskind. The outline of a shattered star of David forms a zigzag which runs symbolically through the history of Berlin.

Die Innenräume im Jüdischen Museum ⟩ sind licht und düster zugleich. Mit diesem ungewöhnlichen Bau ist Daniel Libeskind eine Meisterleistung sinnbildhafter Architektur gelungen.

The rooms within the Jewish Museum are bright and gloomy at the same time. With this extraordinary building Daniel Libeskind created a masterpiece of metaphorical architecture.

‹ Der Chamissoplatz in Kreuzberg mit seinen Stuckfassaden aus dem späten 19. Jahrhundert ist ein Musterbeispiel preußischen Mietskasernenstils: Das Vorderhaus war »gehobenen Ständen« vorbehalten, je tiefer die Hinterhäuser, desto ärmlicher die Bewohner.

The Chamissoplatz in Kreuzberg with its late 19th-century plaster facades is exemplary for the style of Prussian tenements. The flats in the house at the front were meant for the »higher classes«, and the ones further back from the street for the poorer occupants.

≈ Im Viktoriapark mit dem Nationaldenkmal für die Befreiungskriege liegt auch der Kreuzberg, nach dem der Stadtteil benannt ist.

In Viktoriapark, the site of the national monument for the Wars of Liberation, lies the hill named Kreuzberg, from which the district takes its name.

⌃ Die Bergmannstraße bietet heute kulinarische Genüsse aus aller Herren Länder.

In Bergmannstrasse gastronomic delights from all over the world can be sampled.

RUND UM DIE MITTE | AROUND THE CENTRE

‹ Die »Hungerharke«: Das Luftbrückendenkmal am vormaligen innerstädtischen Flughafen Tempelhof erinnert an die Zeit der sowjetischen Blockade der Westsektoren Berlins.

The »Hunger Rake«: the memorial to the Berlin Air Lift at Tempelhof, which used to be the inner-city airport, is a reminder of the Soviet blockade of the western sectors of Berlin.

˄ Von Juni 1948 bis Mai 1949 wurde die Bevölkerung der Westsektoren mit rund 200 000 Versorgungsflügen der Amerikaner und Briten am Leben erhalten. Ein »Rosinenbomber« erhielt einen Ehrenplatz auf dem Gebäude des Deutschen Technikmuseums.

From June 1948 until May 1949 the population of the western sectors survived thanks to approximately 200,000 air deliveries of supplies by the Americans and the British. A »raisin bomber« was given a place of honour in the Deutsches Technikmuseum.

Der Westen
The West

Der Stadtteil Charlottenburg wuchs erst nach der Reichsgründung im Jahre 1871 heran. Zuvor gab es nur den Damm der kurfürstlichen Reiter von Mitte zur Sommerfrische Schloss Charlottenburg (heute Kurfürstendamm). In der Weimarer Republik entwickelte sich der »Neue Westen« immer mehr zum Einkaufs- und Vergnügungszentrum und wurde so zum Synonym der Goldenen Zwanzigerjahre. Nach dem Zweiten Weltkrieg bildeten unter anderem die Bezirke von Charlottenburg bis zur Havel die Westsektoren. »Berlin (West)« wurde zum Symbol des »freien Westens«. Das Geschäftszentrum, die sogenannte City West, erstreckte sich – wie auch heute noch – um den Kurfürstendamm, den Breitscheidplatz und die Tauentzienstraße. Die Mitte der City West markiert die Kaiser-Wilhelm-Gedächtniskirche.

The district of Charlottenburg did not grow until after the foundation of the German Empire in 1871. Before that time, there was only a causeway for the horsemen of the prince electors, leading from the city centre to the summer palace Schloss Charlottenburg (today Kurfürstendamm). In the Weimar Republic the »New West« evolved to become a centre for shopping and amusement, and a synonym for the Golden Twenties. After the Second World War, the districts from Charlottenburg up to the river Havel, among others, formed the Western sectors. »Berlin (West)« became a symbol of the »free West«. The business and shopping area, known as City West, extended, as it does today, around the Kurfürstendamm, Breitscheidplatz and Tauentzienstrasse. The Kaiser Wilhelm Memorial Church marks its centre.

Hoher Symbolgehalt: die Skulptur »Berlin« ›
von Brigitte und Martin Matschinsky-Denninghoff auf der Tauentzienstraße im Herzen des Westens.

Highly symbolic: the sculpture »Berlin« by Brigitte and Martin Matschinsky-Denninghoff on Tauentzienstrasse in the heart of the western part of the city.

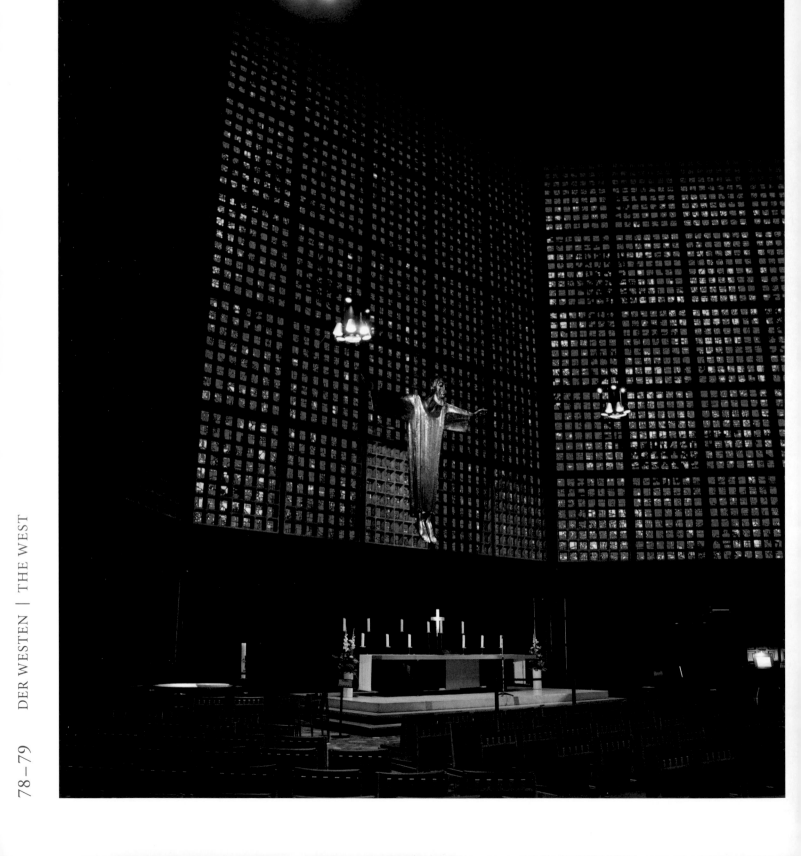

‹ Die Kaiser-Wilhelm-Gedächtniskirche: Der Turmstumpf der kriegszerstörten Kirche blieb als Mahnmal stehen. Der Kirchenneubau von 1961 stammt von Egon Eiermann.

The Kaiser Wilhelm Memorial Church: ravaged by war, the stump of the tower was left in commemoration. The modern church, dating from 1961, was designed by Egon Eiermann.

« Das Kircheninnere mit seinen blauen, wabenartigen Glasfenstern ist erfüllt von meditativer Ruhe.

The church interior with its blue, honeycomb windows creates a mood of meditative peace.

Die Kreuzung Joachimstaler Straße ist der ›
Auftakt zur Flaniermeile Kurfürstendamm
(Ku'damm). Der Ort heißt seit jeher »Kranzlereck« – nach dem berühmten Café. Heute
erinnert noch die Rotunde daran.

The start of the Kurfürstendamm promena-
de (Ku'damm) is the crossroads with Joachimstaler Strasse. This corner has long been
known as »Kranzlereck« after the famous
Café Kranzler. The rotunda is a reminder of
it today.

Das KaDeWe, Kaufhaus des Westens, am ›
Tauentzien ist der wohl größte und schönste Shopping-Tempel Deutschlands.

The department store KaDeWe, Kaufhaus
des Westens, on Tauentzienstrasse is probably the largest and most beautiful temple
of shopping in Germany.

Im eingemauerten West-Berlin war der ›
Bahnhof Zoo der einzige Fernbahnhof.

In walled-in West Berlin, Bahnhof Zoo was
the only station for long-distance trains.

Ab etwa 1900 bot der Ku'damm noble »
Wohnquartiere hinter prächtig-ornamenta-
len Fassaden.

From about 1900 the Ku'damm was a street
of exclusive residences behind superbly or-
namental façades.

‹ Im Theater des Westens, einem wilhelmini-
schen Prunkbau, sind heute Musicals und
Operetten zu Hause.

The Theater des Westens, a magnificent
building from the time of Emperor Wilhelm,
is now a venue for musicals and operettas.

≈ Das Café im Literaturhaus in der Fasanen-
strasse ist ein Ruhepol im Grünen.

The café in the Literaturhaus in Fasanen-
strasse is a restful place with green surround-
ings.

⌃ In den Seitenstraßen des Kurfürstendamms
locken kleine individuelle Geschäfte und
viele schöne Kneipen und Bistros.

In the side streets leading off Kurfürstendamm, small independent shops and many
attractive pubs and bistros can be found.

Das Olympiastadion ist eines der wenigen »
erhaltenen Bauzeugnisse nationalsozialisti-
scher Architektur in Berlin. Zur Fußball-
Weltmeisterschaft 2006 wurde es aufwendig saniert.

The Olympic stadium is one of the few remaining examples of National Socialist architecture in Berlin. It was renovated at
great expense for the football World Cup in
2006.

Das Kongresszentrum ICC stammt aus den »
späten 1970er-Jahren. Es gehört zum Mes-
segelände am Funkturm.

The ICC congress centre dates from the late
1970s. It is part of the trade-fair complex
around the Funkturm, a broadcasting mast.

Als »Stadt in der Stadt« für rund 1300 Be- ›
wohner konzipiert: die »Wohnmaschine«
von Le Corbusier (1957), einem der Meister
der Klassischen Moderne.

Conceived as a »city in the city« for 1,300
residents: the »living machine« by Le Corbusier (1957), a master of Modernist architecture.

Hinter den barocken Fassaden von Schloss «
Charlottenburg (1695–1742) verbergen sich
kunsthistorisch bedeutende Galerien und
prachtvoll ausgestattete Säle.

Behind the Baroque façades of Schloss
Charlottenburg (1695–1742) lie galleries of
great art-historical importance and opu-
lently decorated rooms.

Im weitläufigen Botanischen Garten in Dah- ⌃
lem beeindrucken die »gläsernen Kathe-
dralen« der Gewächshäuser.

The »glass cathedrals« of the hothouses are
impressive features of the extensive Botani-
cal Garden in Dahlem.

Die Philologische Bibliothek der Freien Uni- ⟩
versität in Dahlem stammt von Sir Norman
Foster, der auch das Reichstagsgebäude
umbaute.

The Philological Library of the Freie Univer-
sität in Dahlem was designed by Sir Norman
Foster, who made the alterations to the
Reichstag building.

Außenbezirke und Potsdam
Suburbs and Potsdam

BERLIN

POTSDAM

Berlin ist schön, Berlin ist groß: Zwischen dem Müggelsee im Osten und dem Wannsee im Westen erstrecken sich die unterschiedlichsten Stadtbezirke und Ortsteile mit zahllosen Sehenswürdigkeiten. Das Gesamtgebiet der Stadtgemeinde umfasst zu einem Drittel Wasser, Wald und gestaltete Naturlandschaft: herrliche Naherholungsgebiete für die circa 3,5 Millionen Einwohner der deutschen Metropole. Im Südwesten, hinter der Glienicker Brücke, liegt Potsdam, die Landeshauptstadt Brandenburgs. Für die preußischen Könige war sie Rückzugsort und Garnison. Friedrich Wilhelm I. und sein Sohn, Friedrich der Große, ließen die Stadt zur Residenz ausbauen und die überwältigende Schlösser- und Parklandschaft erschaffen, die heute zum Unesco-Welterbe zählt.

Berlin is big and beautiful: between the lakes Müggelsee in the east and Wannsee in the west lie highly diverse districts of the city with countless sights. One third of the entire area administered by the city government consists of water, forest and natural landscape: wonderful recreational areas for the approximately 3.5 million inhabitants of the largest German city. To the south-west, beyond the Glienicker Brücke, lies Potsdam, capital of the federal state of Brandenburg. For the kings of Prussia it was a retreat and a garrison town. Friedrich Wilhelm I and his son, Frederick the Great, expanded Potsdam to make it their residence and created the breathtaking landscape of palaces and parks that is now a Unesco World Heritage site.

Das restaurierte Schloss Köpenick liegt idyl- › lisch auf einer Insel zwischen Spree und Dahme. 2004 wiedereröffnet, gehört es heute zum Kunstgewerbemuseum.

The restored Schloss Köpenick has an idyllic location on an island between the rivers Spree and Dahme. Reopened in 2004, today it belongs to the Kunstgewerbemuseum.

^ Zentrale Gedenkstätte und Friedhof für
7000 in und um Berlin gefallene Soldaten
der Roten Armee: das Sowjetische Ehrenmal
im Treptower Park.

The central memorial and cemetery for
7,000 soldiers of the Red Army who fell in
and around Berlin: the Soviet monument in
Treptower Park.

⌃ Eine Bronzeskulptur am Rathaus von Köpenick erinnert an den legendären »Hauptmann von Köpenick«.

A bronze sculpture in Köpenick commemorates a legendary figure from literature, the »Captain of Köpenick«.

⌃ Mit über 115 000 Grabstellen ist der Friedhof Weißensee der größte jüdische Friedhof Europas und ein bedeutendes Kulturdenkmal.

With more than 115,000 burials, Weissensee is the largest Jewish cemetery in Europe and an important cultural monument.

Das Strandbad Wannsee mit Strandkörben, ∧
aufgeschütteten Sandstränden und zahlreichen Gaststätten genießt Kultstatus.

The beach on Wannsee with its basket shel-
ters, sand and many places to eat and drink
has cult status.

Auf einer Schiffsfahrt lässt sich die ausge- 〉
dehnte Havelseen-Landschaft, zu der auch
der Große Wannsee gehört, stilgerecht ge-
nießen.

A boat trip is a stylish way to enjoy the lakes
of the river Havel, one of which is Grosser
Wannsee.

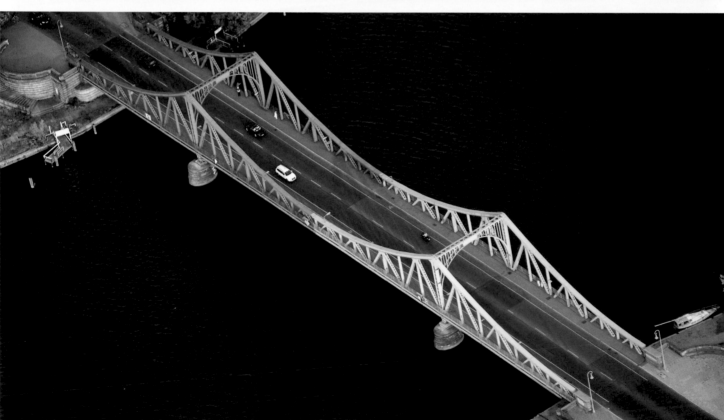

⌐ Die Pfaueninsel, ein Landschaftspark im Berliner Bereich der Havel, gehört zum wald- und wasserreichen Ortsteil Wannsee und ist Teil des Unesco-Welterbes.

Pfaueninsel, a landscaped park in the Berlin district of the Havel, belongs to the Wannsee region of forest and waterways and is part of the Unesco Word Heritage site.

‹ Die Glienicker Brücke zwischen Berlin und Potsdam trennte während des Kalten Krieges die westliche von der östlichen Hemisphäre. Zwischen 1962 und 1986 fanden hier drei Agentenaustauschaktionen statt.

During the Cold War the Glienicker Brücke between Berlin and Potsdam divided the western and eastern blocs. Between 1962 and 1986 three exchanges of agents took place here.

⌃ Den Einsteinturm auf dem Telegrafenberg in Potsdam entwarf Erich Mendelsohn. 1922 als Observatorium erbaut, gilt er heute als Ikone der expressionistischen Architektur.

The Einsteinturm, a tower on the Telegrafenberg hill in Potsdam was designed by Erich Mendelsohn. Built in 1922 as an observatory, it is regarded today as an icon of Expressionist architecture.

⌃ Schloss Sanssouci liegt inmitten ausgedehnter Parkanlagen (heute Unesco-Welterbe) in Potsdam. Das 1745 bis 1747 von Georg Wenzeslaus von Knobelsdorff nach Skizzen Friedrichs des Großen geplante Rokoko-Schloss war Rückzugsort des Königs, der hier 1786 auch starb.

Schloss Sanssouci is surrounded by extensive parks, today classified as a Unesco World Heritage site, in Potsdam. The Rococo palace, built between 1745 and 1747 by Georg Wenzeslaus von Knobelsdorff according to sketches made by Frederick the Great, was a retreat for the king, who died here in 1786.

Potsdam, die Hauptstadt Brandenburgs, »
lässt sich auch vom Schiff aus besichtigen:
Die Kuppel der Nikolaikirche ist weithin
sichtbar. Davor das Alte Rathaus mit einem
vergoldeten Atlas, der die Weltkugel trägt.

Potsdam, the capital of Brandenburg, can
be visited by boat: the dome of the Nikolaikirche is visible from afar. In front of it is the
old town hall with a gilded Atlas bearing
the globe.

Auch Potsdam hat ein Brandenburger Tor: »
Es bildet den Eingang oder Abschluss der
Fußgängerzone.

Potsdam too has a Brandenburg Gate: it is
the entrance to or end of the pedestrian
zone.

Das Holländische Viertel mit seinen Häuser- ›
reihen aus Backstein wurde um 1740 für
niederländische Einwanderer erbaut. De-
ren berufliches Können hat Wirtschaft und
Handwerk in Preußen befördert.

The Dutch Quarter with its rows of brick
houses was built in around 1740 for immi-
grants from the Netherlands. Their profes-
sional skills boosted the economy and
crafts in Prussia.